THE NICHE NARROWS

Praise for *The Niche Narrows*:

"Menashe is an important poet — indeed, I think, one of the most important of his era. . . ."
—P.N. Furbank, *Partisan Review*

"Short, quiet, delicately patterned and mystical, or lyrical in tone, Samuel Menashe's work has seemed to Donald Davie and other discerning critics a major achievement. *The Niche Narrows, New and Selected Poems* gathers several decades of Menashe's verse. . . ." —*Publishers Weekly*

"*The Niche Narrows* . . . should be read by anyone interested in poetry." —Daniel Kane, *Poetry Project Newsletter*

"I can't recommend [*The Niche Narrows*] highly enough."
—M. A. Schaffner, nycbigcitylit.com

"A poet who finds the exact and fewest words to embrace the truths of our condition is too fine for the coarseness of our perceptions, perceptions too often swamped and seduced by our pretentious and noisy culture. That Menashe is not better known in his own country speaks eloquently of the failures of our collective taste."
—Bob Williams, *The Compulsive Reader*

by Samuel Menashe

The Many Named Beloved (1961)
No Jerusalem But This (1971)
Fringe of Fire (1973)
To Open (1974)
Collected Poems (1986)
Penguin Modern Poets, Volume 7 (1996)
The Niche Narrows: New and Selected Poems (2000)

SAMUEL MENASHE

THE NICHE NARROWS

NEW AND SELECTED POEMS

WITH A PREFACE BY DANA GIOIA

TALISMAN HOUSE, PUBLISHERS
JERSEY CITY, NEW JERSEY

Second printing 2002

Published in the United States of America by
Talisman House, Publishers
P.O. Box 3157
Jersey City, New Jersey 07303-3157

Manufactured in the United Sates of America
Printed on acid-free paper

Many of these poems were published in *Penguin Modern Poets (UK)*,
The Sunday Times (London) The New Yorker, Partisan Review,
Times Literary Supplement, The New York Review of Books,
Poetry Nation Review, Temenos, Harper's Magazine,
The Yale Review, The Three Penny Review, Persea 3,
The Antioch Review, and *Commonweal*,
among other publications.

Designed by Samuel Retsov
Text: 12pt Caslon
acid-free paper
Printed by McNaughton & Gunn

Library of Congress Cataloging-in-Publication Data

Menashe, Samuel, 1925-
    The niche narrows : new and selected poems / Samuel Menashe
    p. cm.
    ISBN 1-58498-013-3 (alk. paper) — ISBN 1-58498-012-5 (pbk. : alk. paper)
    I. Title.

PS3563.E47 N53 2000
811'.54--dc21   00-029885

CONTENTS

PREFACE

The public career of Samuel Menashe demonstrates how a serious poet of singular talent, power, and originality can be largely overlooked in our literary culture. There are, of course, several reasons for Menashe's continuing obscurity. He has lived a bohemian life in an age of academic institutionalism. He has not worked as a teacher, editor, or critic—the common paths to literary visibility. But the major cause of his obscurity, I suspect, is strictly literary. Menashe has devoted his entire poetic career to perfecting the short poem—not the conventional short poem of 20-40 lines beloved of magazine editors, but the very short poem. As anyone surveying his *Collected Poems* (1986) will discover, few of his poems are longer than ten lines.

Menashe has not been without his defenders. Almost from the beginning his poems have attracted the attention of some well-known writers. Kathleen Raine, Stephen Spender, Sylvia Townsend Warner, Donald Davie, P. N. Furbank, Austin Clarke, Derek Mahon, Calvin Bedient, and Hugh Kenner have all written appreciatively of his work. The diversity of taste represented by these writers testifies to the wide appeal of Menashe's poems, but it also suggests why their advocacy has proved so ineffective. In the political world of contemporary poetry, it is better to be championed consistently by one literary school than by one critic from each school. Ironically for an American poet, most of his notice has come from England and Ireland, and almost none from New York, his native city. Although Menashe almost never appears in American anthologies, his work has earned a place abroad in the influential Penguin Modern Poets series.

Menashe is essentially a religious poet, though one without an orthodox creed. Nearly every poem he has ever published radiates a heightened religious awareness. His central themes are the unavoidable concerns of religious poetry—the tension between the soul and body, past and present, time and eternity. Like David in the Psalms, his poems are alternately joyous and elegiac. Even his poetic technique—which so strikingly combines imagist compression with traditional rhyme—focuses words into mystical symbols of perception. A reader senses that Menashe's rhymes exist not only for musical effect but also to freeze two or more words in time and hold them perpetually in spiritual or intellectual harmony. (Likewise, his short, dense lines slow down the rhythm to encourage the reader to linger on each word.) Consider the rhymes in this section of "The Bare Tree": "Root of my soul / Split the stone / That holds you— / Be overthrown / Tomb I own." Those two final, unpunctuated lines (only seven syllables long) characterize Menashe's style—not merely compressed and evocative, but talismanic, visionary, and symbolic. He is the most physical poet imaginable. (Note how often he writes about his own body.) But he is a poet who can only understand physical reality in relation to the metaphysical.

If Menashe's spiritual roots are Hebrew, the soil that nourishes them is the English language. His Old Testament is preeminently the King James version, and among his sacred poets is Blake as well as David, Isaiah, and Solomon. He also frequently alludes to the New Testament. His range of allusion is narrow but extraordinarily deep. The Bible permeates his poetry, but he uses it in ways that most readers will immediately understand.

It is futile to lament Menashe's marginality. One notes the injustice and moves on. Better to celebrate the occasion at hand.

Dana Gioia
Santa Rosa, California

THE NICHE NARROWS
NEW AND SELECTED POEMS

Roads run forever
Under feet forever
Falling away
Yet, it may happen that you
Come to the same place again
Stay! You could not do
Anything more certain—
Here you can wait forever
And rejoice at your arrival

WARRIOR WISDOM

Do not scrutinize
A secret wound—
Avert your eyes—
Nothing's to be done
Where darkness lies
No light can come

All my friends are homeless
They do not even have tents
Were I to seek a safe place
I would run nights lost
Ice pelting my face
Sent the wrong way
Whenever I ask—
Afraid to run back,
Each escape the last

Lie down below trees
Be your own guest
Give yourself up . . .
Under this attentive pine
Take your time at noon
The planes will drone by soon

NOVEMBER

Now sing to tarnish and good weathering
A praise of wrinkles which sustain us
Savory as apples whose heaps in attics
Keep many alive through old winter wars

WINTER

For Derek Mahon

I am entrenched
Against the snow,
Visor lowered
To blunt its blow

I am where I go

THE DEAD OF WINTER

In my coat I sit
At the window sill
Wintering with snow
That did not melt
It fell long ago
At night, by stealth
I was where I am
When the snow began

DOWNPOUR

Windowed I observe
The waning snow
As rain unearths
That raw clay—
Adam's afterbirth—
No one escapes
I lie down, immerse
Myself in sleep
The windows weep

APRIL

It is the sun that makes us smile
It is the sun and spring has come
Soon it will reach Norway
Her wooden villages wet
Laughter in each rivulet

APRIL (FOOL)

Stars I leap
Clearing a puddle
Why was I deep
In a muddle?

SUDDEN SHADOW

Crow I scorn you
Caw everywhere
You'll not subdue
This blue air

She who saw the moon last night
She who swayed with the chant
Died in her sleep or dreams—
To say she is dead seems scant.

THE MOMENT OF YOUR DEATH

My head bounces away
In the trough of a wave
You are unbound on your bed
Like water far from a shore
Nothing can reach you now
Not my kiss, not a sound
You are out of hearing
And I have run aground
Where gravel grinds
The face it blinds

THE BARE TREE

My mother once said to me, "When one sees the tree in leaf, one thinks the beauty of the tree is in its leaves, and then one sees the bare tree."

1

Now dry stone holds
Your hopeful head
Your wise brown eyes
And precise nose

Your mouth is dead

2

The silence is vast
I am still and wander
Keeping you in mind
There is never enough
Time to know another

3

Root of my soul
Split the stone
That holds you—
Be overthrown
Tomb I own

4

Darkness stored
Becomes a star
At whose core
You, dead, are

5

I will make you a landscape
Spread forth as waves run

After your death I live
Become a flying fish

MY MOTHER'S GRAVE

Bones
Are mortar
For your wall

Jerusalem

Dust
Upholds
Your street

THE HOST

I am haunted
Out of my house
Gaunt, dispossessed
By the homeless dead
These ghosts, guests
Have bled me white
No marrow is left
In the bone they bite

LANDMARK

I look up to see
Your windows, the house
Standing on this street
Like an old tombstone
Whose dates disappear
I still name you here

I stood, I saw
The room you left
What you could see
The awe of death
Took hold of me

GRIEF

Disbelief
To begin with—
Later, grief
Taking root
Grapples me
Wherever I am
Branches ram
Me in my bed
You are dead

FAMILY PLOT

1

I know that grave
At a stone's throw,
A stone none throws,
That grave outgrown
Like a child's bed

2

I lie in snows
Drifted so high
No one knows
Where I lie

AWAKENING FROM DREAMS

Flung inside out
The crammed mouth
Whose meal I am
Ground, devoured
I find myself now
Benignly empowered

O Lady lonely as a stone—
Even here moss has grown

The friends of my father
Stand like gnarled trees
Yet in their eyes I see
Spring's crinkled leaf

And thus, although one dies
With nothing to bequeath
We are left enough
Love to make us grieve

Always
When I was a boy
I lost things—
I am still
Forgetful—
Yet I daresay
All will be found
One day

FULL FATHOM FIVE

Each new death opens
Old graves and digs
My own grave deeper
The dead, unbound, rise
Wave after wave
I dive for pearls
That were his eyes
But touch bedrock—
Not a coral reef—
Where my father lies
I come to grief

DESCENT

My father drummed darkness
Through the underbrush
Until lightning struck

I take after him

MEMENTO MORI

This skull instructs
Me now to probe
The socket bone
Around my eyes
To test the nose
Bone underlies
To hold my breath
To make no bones
About the dead

NIGHTFALL

Eye this sky
With the mind's eye
Where no light fades
Between the lines
You read at night
Binding that text
Which days divide

MORNING

I wake and the sky
Is there, intact
The paper is white
The ink is black
My charmed life
Harms no one—
No wife, no son

FOREVER AND A DAY

No more than that
Dead cat shall I
Escape the corpse
I kept in shape
For the day off
Immortals take

SELF EMPLOYED

For John Smith

Piling up the years
I awake in one place
And find the same face
Or counting the time
Since my parents died—
Certain less is left
Than was spent—
I am employed
Every morning
Whose ore I coin
Without knowing
How to join
Lid to coffer
Pillar to groin—
Each day hinges
On the same offer

THE ORACLE

Feet east
Head west
Arms spread
North and south
He lies in bed
Intersected
At the mouth

CURRICULUM VITAE

1

Scribe out of work
At a loss for words
Not his to begin with,
The man life passed by
Stands at the window
Biding his time

2

Time and again
And now once more
I climb these stairs
Unlock this door—
No name where I live
Alone in my lair
With one bone to pick
And no time to spare

IN MY DIGS

Caked in a glass
That is clear
Yesterday's dregs
Tell me the past
Happened here

AT A STANDSTILL

For Dana Gioia

That statue, that cast
Of my solitude
Has found its niche
In this kitchen
Where I do not eat
Where the bathtub stands
Upon cat feet—
I did not advance
I cannot retreat

TENEMENT SPRING

1

Blue month of May, make us
Light as laundry on lines
Wind we do not see, mind us
Early in the morning

2

There is a pillow
On the window sill—
Her elbow room—
In the twin window
Enclosed by a grill
Plants in pots bloom
On the window sill

ON THE LEVEL

In the sky's eye test
Does this desk, level
With the window sill,
Uphold my level best
Or is the bed better
For dreams that distill
Words to the letter

A pot poured out
Fulfills its spout

OLD MIRROR

1

In this glass oval
As love's own lake
I face myself, your son
Who looks like you—
Once we were two

2

Ribs ripple skin
Up to the nipples—
Noah, equipped, knew
Every one has two—
This ark I am in
Embarks my twin

OFF THE WALL

Broken mirror off the wall
All of a piece with the past
Whose splinters glint like glass
Stuck in the sole of my shoe—
If I'm out of luck
And down at the heel too
Are seven years enough
Time for me to do?

Pity us
By the sea
On the sands
So briefly

AT MILLAY'S GRAVE

For Eleanor Munro

Your ashes
In an urn
Buried here
Make me burn
For dear life
My candle
At one end—
Night outlasts
Wick and wax
Foe and friend

Take any man
Walking on a road
Alone in his coat
He is a world
No one knows
And to himself
Unknown

Yet, when he wanders most
It is his own way, certain
As spheres astronomers note
In their familiar motion

TELESCOPED

The dead preside
In the mind's eye
Whose lens time bends
For us to see them
As we see the light
Shed by dead stars
Telescopes enlarge

ENLIGHTENMENT

He walked in awe
In awe of light
At nightfall, not at dawn
Whatever he saw
Receding from sight
In the sky's afterglow
Was what he wanted
To see, to know

O Many Named Beloved
Listen to my praise
Various as the seasons
Different as the days
All my treasons cease
When I see your face

PARADISE — AFTER GIOVANNI DI PAOLO

Paradise is a grove
Where flower and fruit tree
Form oval petals and pears
And apples only fair . . .
Among these saunter saints
Who uphold one another
In sacred conversations
Shaping hands that come close
As the lilies at their knees
While seraphim burn
With the moment's breeze

SHADE

Branches spoke
This cupola
Whose leaf inlay
Keeps the sun at bay

JUST NOW

With my head down
Bent to this pen
Which is my plow
I did not see
That little cloud
Above the field—
Unfurrowed brow,
You are its yield

GRAY BOULDER

Gray boulder
Beside the road
You devote me to age
Whose date none decodes
From signs of fire or ice—
Elephant among field mice
You crouched here alone
In the silence of stone

ADAM MEANS EARTH*

I am the man
Whose name is mud
But what's in a name
To shame one who knows
Mud does not stain
Clay he's made of
Dust Adam became—
The dust he was—
Was he his name

*From *Adamah, 'earth' in Hebrew.*

REEDS RISE FROM WATER

rippling under my eyes
Bulrushes tuft the shore

At every instant I expect
what is hidden everywhere

MANNA

For David Curzon

Open your mouth
To feed that flesh
Your teeth have bled
Tongue us out
Bone by bone
Do not allow
Man to be fed
By bread alone

'And He afflicted thee and suffered thee to hunger and fed thee with manna, which thou knewest not neither did thy fathers know, that He might make thee know that man does not live by bread alone, but by every word that proceeds from the mouth of the Lord does man live.' —Deuteronomy VIII:3

PASCHAL WILDERNESS

Blue funnels the sun
Each unhewn stone
Every derelict stem
Engenders Jerusalem

Stone would be water
But it cannot undo
Its own hardness
Rocks might run
Wild as torrents
Plunged upon the sky
By cliffs none climb

Who makes fountains
Spring from flint
Who dares tell
One thirsting
There's a well

PROMISED LAND

At the edge
Of a world
Beyond my eyes
Beautiful
I know Exile
Is always
Green with hope—
The river
We cannot cross
Flows forever

If I were as lean as I feel
Only my bones would show
Living bone, ideal—
Without a shadow—
For the exacting dance
That the Law commands
Until I overstepped
The forbidden ark
To take on flesh
Wrestling in the dark

THE SHRINE WHOSE SHAPE I AM

The shrine whose shape I am
Has a fringe of fire
Flames skirt my skin

There is no Jerusalem but this
Breathed in flesh by shameless love
Built high upon the tides of blood
I believe the Prophets and Blake
And like David I bless myself
With all my might

I know many hills were holy once
But now in the level lands to live
Zion ground down must become marrow
Thus in my bones I am the King's son
And through death's domain I go
Making my own procession

As the tall, turbaned
Black, incense man
Passed the house
I called after him
And ran out to the street
Where at once we smiled
Seeing one another
And without a word
Like a sword that leaps from its lustrous sheath
He was swinging his lamp with abundant grace
To my head and to my heart and to my feet . . .
Self-imparted we swayed
Possessed by that One
Only the living praise

'The dead do not praise Thee.' —Psalm of David

OLD AS THE HILLS

The lilt of a slope
Under the city
Flow of the land
With streets in tow
Where houses stand
Row upon row

DUSK

night
into
earth
from
rise
Voices

NIGHT WALK

For John Thornton

In eyes of strangers glimpsed
On the street at night
I see more than meets the eye
In the broad daylight

The circumspect passer-by
Keeps to himself, and yet
His eyes give him the lie
At once when they are met

The scrutiny
Of a chicken's eye
Terrifies me—
What does it think?
Not brain but beak
Chills my blood—
It stares to kill

RURAL SUNRISE

Furrows erupt
Like spokes of a wheel
From the hub of the sun—
The field is overrun—
No rut lies fallow
As shadows yield
Plow and bucket
Cart and barrow

WATERFALL

For Kate Farrell

Water falls
Apart in air
Hangs like hair
Light installs
Itself in strands
Of water falling
The cliff stands

A flock of little boats
Tethered to the shore
Drifts in still water
Prows dip, nibbling

TWILIGHT

For Clare Carroll

Looking across
The water we are
Startled by a star—
It is not dark yet
The sun has just set

Looking across
The water we are
Alone as that star
That startled us,
And as far

Eaves at dusk
beckon us
to peace
whose house,
espoused,
we keep

STAR-CROSSED

This lunar air
Draws me to you,
The moon's magnet
Aligns that pair
Whom dragons slew,
Whose course was set
Before they knew

SOLITUDE

Awake I see
The simple nose
Pathetic feet
Of one asleep

WESTERN WIND

One hand cold
One hand hot
One turns pages
One does not
As I lie in bed
Reading poems . . .
Remembering how
You love this one
I've come to now
My arms are numb

DREAMING

Windswept
as the sea
at whose ebb
I fell asleep,
dreams collect
in the shell
that is left,
perfecting it.

THE SANDPIPER

The sandpiper
Scampers over sand
Advances, withdraws
As breakers disband

Each wave undergoes
The bead of his eye
He pecks what it tows
Keeps himself dry

ON MY BIRTHDAY

For Chris Agee

I swam in the sea our mother
Naked as the day I was born
Still fit at forty-four
Willing to live forever

SKETCHES: BY THE SEA

1

That black man running
Headlong on the beach
Throws back the white
Soles of his feet
Lightning strikes
Twice on the sand
Left foot and right,
My pen in hand

2

Hearing the sea
Not seeing it
On the other side
Of the dunes
Is enough for me
This morning
The distance I keep
From the sea I hear
Brings distance near

3

At night, off shore
Sometimes the lights
On the fishing boats
Sink out of sight
That string of lights
Salt water wets
Makes the fish rise
To tridents and nets

DOMINION

Stare at the sea
you on your chair
sinking in sand,
Command the waves
to stand like cliffs,
Lift up your hand

So they stood
Upon ladders
With pruning hooks
Backs to the king
Who took his leave
Of gardening

This morning
I am forlorn
As he was then
No one born
After the war
Remembers when

LE LAC SECRET

For Paul Keegan

They have now traced me to my uncles
One died a beggar in a room with no windows
And one danced until he was undone, like Don Juan
Though they try to find me out, I am still as the swan
While those who search grow grim
And darker in their doubt

SURVIVAL

I stand on this stump
To knock on wood
For the good I once
Misunderstood

Cut down, yes
But rooted still
What stumps compress
No axe can kill

WALKING STICK

This stick springs
When you lean on it
It is still green
You can feel the sap
This stick gives
A spring to your walk
Old sticks snap
This stick bends like a bow
You are the arrow

TO OPEN

Spokes slide
Upon a pole
Inside
The parasol

SCISSORS

Sharpen your wit—
Each half of it—
Before you shut
Scissors to cut

Shear skin deep
Underneath wool
Expose the sheep
Whose leg you pull

SPUR OF THE MOMENT

His head rears back
Cresting upon his neck
His uplifted legs prance
As he champs at the bit
The unbridled rider sits
With reins in hand
Astride this dance
He is saddled with

SIMON SAYS

In a doorway
Staring at rain
Simple withstands
Time on his hands

Using the window ledge
As a shelf for books
Does them good—
Bindings are belts
To be undone,
Let the wind come—
Hard covers melt,
Welcome the sun—
An airing is enough
To spring the lines
Which type confines,
But for pages uncut
Rain is a must.

THE ANNUNCIATION

She bows her head
Submissive, yet
Her downcast glance
Asks the angel, "Why,
For this romance,
Do I qualify?"

NIGHT MUSIC
(Pizzicato)

Why am I so fond
Of the double bass
Of bull frogs
(Or do I hear the prongs
Of a tuning fork,
Not a bull fiddle)
Responding—
In perfect accord—
To one another
Across this pond
How does each frog know
He is not his brother
Which frog to follow
Who was his mother
(Or is it a jew's harp
I hear in the dark?)

FAMILY SILVER

That spoon fell out
Of my mother's mouth
Before I was born,
But I was endowed
With a tuning fork

IMPROVIDENCE

Owe, do not own
What you can borrow
Live on each loan
Forget tomorrow
Why not be in debt
To one who can give
You whatever you need
It is good to abet
Another's good deed

SALT AND PEPPER

For Calvin Bedient

Here and there
White hairs appear
On my chest—
Age seasons me
Gives me zest—
I am a sage
In the making
Sprinkled, shaking

INFANT, OLD MAN

Up in arms
That hold her high
Enough to bend
Her father's ear
She babbles by
Me on a bench
At my wit's end.

PIRATE

For P. N. Furbank

Like a cliff
My brow hangs over
The cave of my eyes
My nose is the prow of a ship

I plunder the world

CARGO

For Rachel Hadas

Old wounds leave good hollows
Where one who goes can hold
Himself in ghostly embraces
Of former powers and graces
Whose domain no strife mars—
I am made whole by my scars
For whatever now displaces
Follows all that once was
And without loss stows
Me into my own spaces

VOYAGE

Water opens without end
At the bow of a ship
Rising to descend
Away from it

Days become one
I am who I was

SHEEN

Sun splinters
In water's skin
Quivers hundreds
Of lines to rim
One radiance
You within

AT CROSS PURPOSES

1

Is this writing mine
Whose name is this
Did I underline
What I was to miss?

2

An upheaval of leaves
Enlightens the tree
Rooted it receives
Gusts on a spree

3

Beauty makes me sad
Makes me grieve
I see what I must leave

4

Scaffold, gallows
Do whose will
Who hallows wood
To build, kill

5

Blind man, anvil
No hammer strikes
Your eyes are spikes

FIRE DANCE

Must smiles subside in a sigh
And sobs underlie laughter
Shall we always leap high
With flames leaping after

TRANSPLANT

I would give
My liver, kidneys
Heart itself
For you to live
In perfect health
With me, your clone
Whose grafted cells
Grow marrow, bone

If all else fails
Do not reject
My skin or nails
Whatever's left
Of me for you
By a hair's breadth
Will see us through

THE LIVING END

Before long the end
Of the beginning
Begins to bend
To the beginning
Of the end you live
With some misgivings
About what you did.

NIGHT WATCH

For William Jay Smith

The heart I hear in bed tonight
Is mine—it frightens me
To hear my heart so clearly
It could stop at any time

Keep your ear to the ground
I was told without fear
Now I am hollowed for sound
And it is my heart I hear

SLEEP

gives wood its grain
Dreams knot the wood

DREAMS

For Katharine Washburn

What wires lay bare
For this short circuit
Which makes filaments flare—
Can any bulb resist
Sockets whose threads twist
As fast as they are spun—
Who conducts these visits
Swifter than an eclipse
When the moon is overcome?

HOME MOVIE

Awake at once
No space between
The day and dream
Seen as it runs
Me off the screen
No time to splice
Slices of life—
I'm wide awake,
No second take.

INKLINGS

Inklings *sans* ink
Cling to the dry
Point of the pen
Whose stem I mouth
Not knowing when
The truth will out

WHAT TO EXPECT

At death's door
The end in sight
Is life, not death
Each breath you take
Is breathtaking

Save your breath
Does not apply—
You must die.

THE VISITATION

His body ahead
Of him on the bed
He faces his feet
Sees himself dead,
A corpse complete
With legs and chest
And belly between
Swelling the scene
Of the crime you left,
Taking your time,
Angel of Death

RED GLINTS IN BLACK HAIR

It is the rose below white
Gold suns under sea green
A nose formed for insight
Things visible but unseen
Keeping my eyes to the king
As I call wise night my queen

A BRONZE HEAD

For Barry Ahearn

He's in his garden now
Sticking his neck out
Of a flower bed,
A head without shoulders

We are not statues yet
Nor about to become
Immortals, thoroughbreds
At the starting post
Programmed to run
A race against ghosts
Whose inside track
Stakes out the hindmost
For us, taken aback
By the prowess we lack.

ANONYMOUS

Truth to tell,
Seldom told
Under oath,
We live lies
And grow old
Self disguised—
Who are you
I talk to?

EYES

For Geordie Greig

Eyes have their day
Before the tongue
That slips to say
What they see at once
Without word play,
Betraying no one

Be deaf, dumb, a dunce
With cleft palate
Bereft of speech
Open eyes possess
That wilderness
No tongue can breach

French spoken
across the snow
on Sheep Meadow
evokes a very rich hour
of the Duke of Berry . . .
three men traversing
a field of snow—
one of them alone—
hedged by trees
on the south side
where the towers
of the city rise . . .
one of those hours
in early afternoon
when nothing happens
but time makes room

SUNSET, CENTRAL PARK

A wall of windows
Ignited by the sun
Burns in one column
Of fire on the lake
Night follows day
As embers break

AUTUMN

1

I walk outside the stone wall
Looking into the park at night
As armed trees frisk a windfall
Down paths that lampposts light

2

Streets at night like decks
With spars overhead
Whose rigging ropes
Stars into scope

AWAKENING

Like one born again
To the same mother
I wake each morning
The same, another
Who takes my name
But cannot place me
In dreams, nightmares
Where I became
The one she bears

SOMEONE WALKED OVER MY GRAVE

The breath breaks a cold shuddered hollow
That instant, unbearably, I know
The beauty of this world

Those lips the young man my father
Found more fair than the bud of a rose
Now almost touched to dust—kiss that dust
You trod God of Life, God of the world

THE NICHE

The niche narrows
Hones one thin
Until his bones
Disclose him

HALLELUJAH

Eyes open to praise
The play of light
Upon the ceiling—
While still abed raise
The roof this morning
Rejoice as you please
Your Maker who made
This day while you slept,
Who gives grace and ease,
Whose promise is kept.

'Let them sing for joy upon their beds.' —Psalm 149

THE SPRIGHT OF DELIGHT

For Kathleen Raine

The spright of delight
Springs, summersaults
Vaults out of sight
Rising, self-spun
Weight overcome

A-
round
my neck
an amu-
let
Be-
tween
my eyes
a star
A
ring
in my
nose
and a
gold
chain
to
Keep me
where
You
are
    *